50 Graded Studies for Rec

Selected and edited by Sally Adams & Paul Harris

CONTENTS

FABER *ff* MUSIC

© 2004 by Faber Music Ltd
First published in 2004 by Faber Music Ltd
Bloomsbury House 74–77 Great Russell Street London WC1B 3DA
Music processed by Jackie Leigh
Cover design by Shireen Nathoo Design
Printed in England by Caligraving Ltd
All rights reserved

ISBN10: 0-571-52318-8
EAN13: 978-0-571-52318-4

To buy Faber Music publications or to find out about the full range of titles available
please contact your local music retailer or Faber Music sales enquiries:

Faber Music Limited, Burnt Mill, Elizabeth Way, Harlow CM20 2HX
Tel: +44 (0)1279 82 89 82   Fax: +44 (0)1279 82 89 83
sales@fabermusic.com   fabermusic.com

INTRODUCTION

In this collection we have assembled a broad repertoire of study material that covers a wide spectrum of basic technique and provides a firm foundation for progress. The studies are arranged in order of increasing difficulty, according to a carefully planned technical progression – ranging from Preparatory Test to Grade 5.

In the main, we have drawn on established study collections for the recorder, alongside some arrangements of appropriate flute and oboe study repertoire. We have also included a number of new, specially-composed studies that introduce aspects of 20th century style and thus extend the scope of the selection.

It is important to identify – perhaps with the assistance of your teacher – the specific purpose of each study and the particular facets of technique it sets out to develop. The following suggestions will be helpful.

Breath control Most aspects of tonal control depend on a sustained and concentrated column of air. This is the basis of all legato and staccato playing, and a means of controlling intonation.

Tone quality It is important to maintain quality and consistency of tone when playing studies, scales and technical exercises.

Dynamics While the actual volume of sound implied by particular dynamic markings may vary from work to work, dynamic relationships within a single study should be constant as far as possible. Subtle gradations of dynamic such as *crescendo* and *diminuendo* are not expected of the beginner, but by the end of this book should be well-projected – increasing or decreasing at a constant rate. Where dynamic markings are lacking, editorial dynamics have been added as a guide; in these instances you are also encouraged to add your own in accordance with the style of the period.

Intonation When practising studies, it is important to test intervals by reference to a tuning fork, piano or electronic tuning device.

Articulation The chosen length and quality of notes should be matched throughout and related to the character of the particular study. An understanding of the various symbols used is necessary.

Finger technique The development of a controlled and co-ordinated finger movement is the main purpose of the technical study. You should always identify the particular difficulties and seek to acquire the necessary control.

Rhythm Where there are rhythmic difficulties, sub-divide the basic pulse. You should always count, but it is important that undue emphasis is not placed on beats, except for a slight feeling for the natural bar accents. These primary and secondary accents should be felt but not over-emphasized.

Character The character and mood of a study should be considered, as these will determine note duration, accentuation, tone-colour and so on.

PAUL HARRIS
SALLY ADAMS

LIST OF SOURCES

The studies in this book are drawn from the following sources:

Jacques Aubert (1689–1753)	*Les amuzettes* (c.1733)
Joseph de Boismortier (1689–1755)	*Diverses pièces pour une flûte traversière seule* (Paris, 1728)
Jules Demersseman (1833–1866)	*The Art of Phrasing* Op.4
Jacob van Eyck (c.1589/90–1657)	*Der fluiten-lusthof* (Amsterdam, 1646)
Gewin Fetzen	*Studies* (Berlin, 1922)
Jean-Pierre Freillon-Poncein (1655–1720)	*La veritable manière* (Paris, 1700)
Giuseppe Gariboldi (1833–1905)	*Method for Flute* (Paris, 1870)
Gustav Hinke	*Praktische Elementarschule* (Leipzig, 1888)
Jacques-Martin Hotteterre (1674–1763)	*Methode pour la musette* (Paris, 1737)
Ernesto Köhler (1849–1907)	*Schule für Flöte* (Leipzig, 1887)
John Playford (1623–1686)	*The English Dancing Master* (London, 1728)
Emil Prill.	*Schule für Böhmflöte* Op.7 (Leipzig, 1904)
Jean-Louis Tulou (1786–1865)	*Méthode de flûte* Op.100 (Paris, 1835)
Erasmus Widmann (1572–1634)	*Musicalischer Tungendtspiegel* (Nuremberg, 1613)
Ludwig Wiedemann	*69 Studies* (Berlin, 1890)

1
King Richard, his delight

Paul Harris

2

Sally Adams

3
A lovely lass to a friar came
from The Beggar's Opera

Anon.

© 2004 by Faber Music Ltd.

This music is copyright. Photocopying is ILLEGAL.

6

7
Lavignone

Jacob van Eyck

10

Rumsey's round *or* In the turtle soup

Paul Harris

11
Rosina
(Allemande)

Erasmus Widmann

12

Gustav Hinke

13

Gavotte 'La pointilleuse'

Joseph Bodin de Boismortier

14

The Quaker's grace

John Playford

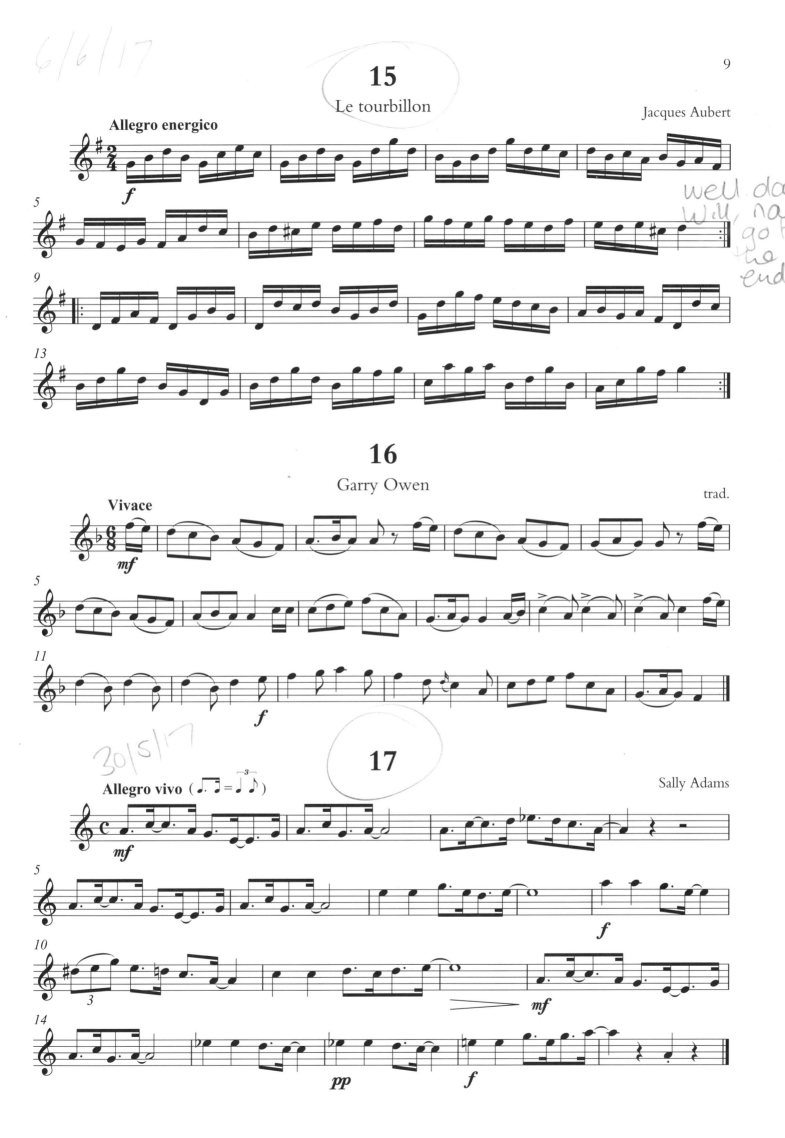

15

Le tourbillon

Jacques Aubert

16

Garry Owen

trad.

17

Sally Adams

18

Emil Prill

19

Al hebben de Princen haren

Jacob van Eyck

20

Air irlandais

Jules Demersseman

21

Gewin Fetzen

22

Giuseppe Gariboldi

23

'Twas within a furlong of Edinburgh Town

John Playford

24

Gustav Hinke

14

25

La bergère

Jacob van Eyck

26

Ernesto Köhler

27

Gavotte

Anon.

28

Ludwig Wiedemann

29

Fred's frolic

Sally Adams

30

The devil amang the tailors

trad.

31

Jean-Pierre Freillon-Poncein

32

Lumps of pudding

John Playford

18

33
The Joker

Esprit Philippe Chédeville

34
A littlemore, a littleless

Paul Harris

35

Wat zal men op den Avond doen

Jacob van Eyck

36

Giuseppe Gariboldi

37

Sally Adams

38

Jean-Louis Tulou

39

Engels Nachtegaeltje

Jacob van Eyck

40
Rondeau

Joseph Bodin de Boismortier

24

41

Csárdás

Ludwig Wiedemann

42

Franz Blatt

43

Bourrée

Jacques-Christophe Naudot

44

Oswald's frolick

Paul Harris

45

Giuseppe Gariboldi

46

Prelude

Georg Philipp Telemann

47

Friedrich Kuhlau

48

Artemis dances

Sally Adams

49

Nicolas Dôthel

50

Lord Gillingwater of Queen Square

Paul Harris